J. Dyer Ball

Five Thousand Years of John Chinaman

Salzwasser

J. Dyer Ball

Five Thousand Years of John Chinaman

1. Auflage | ISBN: 978-3-84604-832-0

Erscheinungsort: Frankfurt, Deutschland

Erscheinungsjahr: 2020

Salzwasser Verlag GmbH

Reprint of the original, first published in 1906.

Five Thousand Years

of

John Chinaman,

by

J. Dyer Ball, M.R.A.S., &c.

HONGKONG:

KELLY & WALSH, LD.
Shanghai, Singapore, Yokohama.

1906.

To
SIR MATTHEW NATHAN, K.C.M.G.,
WHOSE
KINDLY APPRECIATION
ON
THE TWO OCCASIONS HE HEARD THIS LECTURE
HAS ENCOURAGED THE AUTHOR
TO PUBLISH IT.

PREFACE.

This lecture was first delivered to the Odd Volumes, Society in the City Hall, Hongkong, on the 22nd November 1904. After which it was repeated at the Literary Club, Union Church, Hongkong, on the 9th February 1905; and again at the Y. M. C. A. on the 11th October 1905.

Its favourable reception has encouraged the lecturer to provide it now with a larger audience.

A few alterations and additions have been made.

FIVE
THOUSAND YEARS
OF
JOHN CHINAMAN.

It is a bold task to attempt to try and give within an hour's space, an account of 5,000 or more years of a people's history.   It is, of course, impossible to do justice to such an immense subject in such a limited time.   What I propose is to use a thin, attenuated thread of history to guide one's course down the ages and to strike off now and then on one subject, which amongst numbers of others may appear of interest. Long gaps must be left—some dynasties will be passed over unnoticed and thousands upon thousands of interesting episodes and events frought with lasting benefit or woe to the nation and its people completely ignored.   I trust, however, that there will be enough left to give some idea of the history of the race and of the numerous problems to be studied and facts to be unearthed during the 5,000 years of their life.

I have then simply taken 5,000 years as the time to pass under our review in a cursory survey to-night, though the Chinese carry their records back far beyond that.   We perhaps laugh at such a remote antiquity; but our scientific men are constantly pushing back the probable geological period when the human race came on to the scene and adding to the possible æon-long age of what is otherwise, as regards the individual, a short-lived life.   So though we cannot accept the so-called facts of the Chinese legend writer as veritable occurrences when narrated by him concerning these remote periods, the number of years of which these ages are composed are not so absurd as at first sight might appear to be the case.   Take, for example the recent discoveries regarding ancient Babylon and Egypt and their extinct civilisations. One savant has recently stated that they may date back 30,000 years 'and that agriculture by migratory tribes may extend back 30,000 years more': so that the Chinese mythologist and the Western modern scientist are not so far apart in their estimates.

If it is interesting for an individual to trace up his own family history back a few generations or centuries, how much more so is it for one to turn one's attention to that of the aggregate of the individual, as represented by the people, or nation, and trace their antecedents up for thousands of years till certain knowledge is lost in the mists of antiquity. With modern Western nations we soon lose our way in our attempt to penetrate the past history of our race; but with Eastern nations, while the man of the West has come and gone, they have lasted for almost countless generations: they have continued to exist through millenniums after millenniums, while countless mushroom empires have sprung up in a night, as it were, and gone, like Jonah's gourd, under the fierce heat of the sun of adversity.

It is almost with a feeling of awe that one approaches a hoary antiquity like this. It is like leaving the busy, bustling streets and entering the quiet precincts of some old-world fane. The noise of the modern world with its present-day civilisation vibrates in the air; but its insistent roar is subdued as it beats against the thick walls until it sounds like the distant murmur of a far-off shore.

To think that for thousands of years this people have lived in this land and, having evolved a system of government and civilisation, which was well suited for them and conducive to stability, they have prospered themselves and left the world immediately round them the better for their advent into it. And all the time the Western world with its insistent clamour and bustling moods has made but little impression on them: the walls of exclusion have shut out all but the faintest murmur of modern civilisation and progress. In the Middle Kingdom this mighty mass of people has been self-centred; their civilisation was superior to that of the wild nomadic tribes on their northern frontiers; they looked down with disdain on the barbarous races that lived on their western and southern boundaries. The ocean washed their eastern shores, but, while for many a century it served as a bulwark to keep off the foe, it also formed a highway for the more skilled Chinese to travel to the Malayan peninsular, to Siam, to Bangkok, to India, and even to the Red Sea.

Speculation is rife as to where this wonderful people came from. A Babylonian or Accadian origin is suggested, and there appear many points of similarity between that of the ancient civilisation on the banks of the Euphrates and that of China; but one would like more certain ground to go upon before definitely accepting this as the source from which the Chinese were derived. One must speak with a considerable amount of doubt on the subject; we have no certain ground to go upon, and as long as sober common-sense guides us, we must for the present be content to let their original habitat remain a mystery, till perchance science in its investigations has hit upon some solution of the mystery, or discovered sufficient facts to turn surmises into certitude.

Wild are the fancies of the Chinese themselves as to their ancient history. In common with all people they push its limits back so far that it is finally projected on to a plain beyond the present ken of mortal men, and gods reign supreme, and divine beings shape the course of the world, evolving out of their inner consciousness for the benefit of man, such inventions as sleep. Some doctors of late are saying that we do not sleep enough, and that many of the ills to which flesh is heir are due to a want of that blessed boon; but picture to yourselves what the condition of man must have been before sleep was invented at all.

'The date of the beginning of all things has been nicely calculated by Chinese chronologists,' says one interesting writer on Chinese subjects. 'There was first of all a period when nothing existed, though some enthusiasts have attempted to deal with a period antecedent to that.' Such a time would appear to be beyond our power to picture; the mind refuses to grasp it; and language to describe it. Something; nothing; before nothing, what? 'Gradually nothing took upon itself the form and limitations of unity, represented by a point in the centre of a circle, an Aura, a Zeitgeist, or whatever one may please to call it.' Our scientists in the West have long puzzled about the age of the world, but the Chinese have settled the question for us. The author we have just quoted goes on to say that, "After countless ages, spent apparently in doing nothing, his Monad split into two Principles, one active, the other passive; one positive the other negative; light and darkness; male and female. The interaction of these two principles resulted in the production of all things, as we see them in the universe around us [I pray you to mark the time] 2,269,881 years ago.' (Our geologists say 100,000,000) Do not forget the one year, I beg of you: it is so important.

But let us get to something more substantial than these wild fancies, on to some solid ground instead of such vagaries. The Kwun Lun Mountains divide Tibet from Tartary and it has been thought that probably on the north side of these mountains the future Chinese resided for some time before they finally proceeded on the last stages of their long journey to the future China.

It is said that there are two races in China. The older race was darker; the newer race was fairer. The latter were the new comers. There was a certain blending of the two. And doubtless we have a proof that the Chinese at one time were fairer then they are now, for, as any of you can see, Chinese babies and little children have fairer hair than the grown-up people. Especially will you notice this if the sun shines through the youngster's locks, for it will readily be seen then that there is a brown tinge to them. Again may we not take it as a sign also that such was the case from the fact that in reality the Chinese, both men and women, admire the fairer faces of our women-kind? Conversation with them will elicit the fact. I have even heard of an Amah admiring the foreign baby she was nurse to, because it was so fair. Then the Chinese ladies are fond of powdering their brownish-yellow faces, especially was this the case a few years ago when powdering was more in fashion than now and it was then applied indiscriminately all over the face. Then you will find at the little shrine at the Adam and Eve, or Padre's Rock, above the Bowen Road, in this Colony, that the women, who frequent that little temple and whose faces are their fortune, smear the idol plentifully with white powder, hoping that it may cause their own faces to be white and beautiful; other things also seem to lend confirmation to the view.

About 2,700 years before Christ we find the Chinese in China. They had probably come by some north-western passage, not by sea, but by land, doubtless attracted by the fertile plains of North China. They were, however, not the first to set foot in this land, for they were preceded by the aborigines—there were races living in China before the Chinese—China was not a lone land o'er which the foot of man had never trod. There were inhabitants in China before the Chinese; but we do not call them Chinese; we are content to style them aborigines. When they came we cannot say, the Chinese found them here when they came. It seems to be an axiom in this world that everybody comes from somewhere else than where you find him, such a reputation the human race has for wandering.

One must speak with a certain amount of caution with the insufficient data there is to go upon; but it is very probable that the Chinese race only formed one of several numerous waves of immigration into the land—they were preceded by others and doubtless followed by others; but owing to the advanced civilisation the race we call the Chinese brought with them, and owing also to their admirable powers of organisation, they were either able to engulf some of these other races into their body politic, or they drove them gradually before them into the mountain fastnesses some of them now occupy, or they left them in possession of tracts of land from which they could not oust them. Instances of the latter case are to be found in many provinces in China, and one of the former we have in our very midst here in the South of China in our boat population in Hongkong, Macao, and Canton, who were originally an aboriginal race. To this date they differ in some of their customs and in the pronunciation of some of their words. A few of their old-time words have also survived in the every-day speech of these descendants of a former tribe, race, or nation, of whom little seems to be known unfortunately. Though this boat population is allowed to remain on the land, or rather on the water, they are looked down upon by the genuine landsmen, who are the descendants of the Chinese settlers—this feeling is carried so far that intermarriages, as a rule, are not common between the two races.

To summarise:—The mythological period of the Chinese covers from 45,000 to 500,000 years and commences with the creation of the world when P'ún Kwú separated with his hammer and chisel the skies and the earth which were sticking together. Whatever P'ún Kwú may have been originally, he must have been a giant by the time his more than Herculean labours were finished, for he rose to his work, growing six feet every day. He must have fed on the food of the gods. On his death his head became mountains, his breath wind and clouds, his limbs were changed into the four poles; his veins into rivers; his sinews into the undulations of the earth's surface; and his flesh into fields; his beard, like Berenice's hair, was turned into stars; his skin and hair into herbs and trees; and his teeth, bones, and marrow into metals, rocks, and precious stones; his dropping sweat increased to rain; and lastly the insects which stuck to his body were transformed into people. A fine origin for the human race!!! Some people will insist that Darwin said we were descended from monkeys. But here is no mistake. No wonder the Chinese are tender and patient with the animated life they support so often on their own bodies!!! According to this story these insects are their own ancestors.

P'ún Kwú's labours lasted for 18,000 years and he was succeeded by three sovereigns, the Celestial, the Terrestial, and the Human who reigned for another 18,000 years. It was then that sleep was invented, and men learned to eat and drink. One is curious to know how they existed before these inventions; but that, I am afraid, we shall never learn. After this two more sovereigns came and one of them brought down fire from heaven, and mankind had the blessing of cooked dishes.

After this highly interesting period, we come to the legendary history, or the ancient history of China. It starts with Fu-hi and the five kings who followed him are called the Five Sovereigns. Here are three dates for Fu-hi's reign—you can take any you like, it does not matter much. They are B.C. 2,852, 2,953, or 3,322. This is about the same time as the commencement of the Assyrian monarchy. Amongst other blessings conferred at this time was marriage. Fu-hi had seven successors, 747 years covers the time of these eight kings. There is a good deal of the mythical about it all, as you may well suppose; but with the discoveries that have been made in recent years in Egypt and some other ancient lands, I think we are getting less sceptical of everything connected with the early ages of the world. The practice of agriculture and the invention of wheeled vehicles belong to this period. It is only now that energetic steps are being taken in England and her colonies for the introduction of the metric system; but, if we are to believe the Chinese, it was at this time that a decimal system of weights and measures was introduced.

Hwang-ti was the great emperor who is said to have regulated the calendar and introduced the cycle of sixty years which is still in use in China. He is said to have been the founder of the great empire, and his dominions extended as far south as the Yang-tsz.

'The Chinese had some knowledge of astronomy before progress is known to have been made with the science in Europe.' Hwang-ti published an edict about the year 2,600 B.C. in which his mathematical tribunal were told 'whether the instant of the occurrence of any celestial phenomenon was erroneously, or the phenomenon itself not, foreseen or predicted either negligence should be punished with death.' Not long after we are told Ho and Hi suffered death on the ground that an eclipse had occurred which they had not foreseen.

Notwithstanding the doubt and disparagement thrown on early Chinese inventions by some, no one has been found bold enough to try and wrest the palm from them for the three discoveries of porcelain, lacquer-ware, and the manufacture of silk. The latter is of very ancient orgin; it is referred to in the Shi King, one of the oldest of the Chinese Classics. Silkworms, it is said, were first reared by the Empress of Hwang-ti (B.C. 2,600). She has been deified and worshipped as the Goddess of Silk. It is utterly impossible to say how much silk is used in China now; but the Chinese consider that their own consumption is double that of the amount exported. China of late, being forced into the comity of nations, is building up a national debt, and the chief asset for meeting the several loans which go to form this debt is her silk and its products. Half of the total value of her export trade was silk and its products in the sixties. Of late from various causes it has sunk to 35 per cent.

But to return to ancient times; we jump over 240 years and arrive at China's golden Age when the two great Emperors Yao and Shun lived and reigned—two of China's greatest sages, as they are considered to be. They are indebted to Confucius and Mencius, to a great extent, for the

very high position they hold in the estimation of the Chinese.
It would be perhaps nearer the truth to look upon them
as more holding the position of chieftains than of great
emperors ruling over enormous tracts of land.

Interesting as it might be to enlarge on these wonderful times, we must pass on and we come to the great Yü.
The empire first became hereditary in his family; and we
may consider him as the first sovereign of the Chinese
nation, and with him the dynasty of Há commenced
(2205-1818 B.C.).   Roads on land and vessels for the path-
less sea were made by this monarch, as well as for the
narrower channels of the inland waters.   The idea of boats
was said to be first derived from leaves floating on water,
or from the sight of driftwood, or again, another account
says, they were derived by natural development from the
more primitive raft; but still another story is to the effect
that a woman who kept her eyes open and her brain active,
evolved the idea of oars for her first venture, a raft, from
the fins of a fish, which she watched while washing clothes
one day in the river.   The tail of the fish also suggested
the rudder, or what is perhaps more likely the yíu-lò, or long
stern scull, of the Chinese.   This wonderful inventive
genius is now said to be one of the Taoist eight genii, the
only woman amongst the eight.   If that is the case, she
well deserves the honour.

It was in this dynasty that chop-sticks were first used,
a decided improvement on the employment of the fingers.
The Chinese spoon looks as if it were copied from the
lotus leaf.

The great Yü is renowned for the great and wonderful engineering skill with which he drained away the
overflowing floods of a terrible inundation and confined
the waters to their proper limits.   For eight long years
did he toil at this stupendous task; and so absorbed was
he in these labours, 'that though he thrice passed his door,
and on one occasion heard the wailing of his own child, he
never entered till the completion of his task.'   But for the
great Yü, the Chinese historian, in the most cold-blooded
manner suggests a most awful fate for the race.   For says
he but for Yü we might all have been fishes.   I do not know
that even Darwin has suggested this horrible chance in our
development—of degenerating into a fish or even an ascidian
perchance, when actually arrived at man's estate on our

upward course from a primitive oyster or something equally low, or lower even, in the scale of existence.

Yü was a wise sovereign. It was in his reign that the discovery of spirits—ardent spirits was made, for other spirits had evidently been discovered long before. The spirits were distilled from various grains by a man name Yi-ti. The great Yü tasted samples brought to him and, though he liked the taste of them, he professed himself much distressed at the discovery, saying, with true prophetic instinct, 'the days will come when some of my successors through drinking this will cause infinite sorrow to the nation.' After which he expelled Yi-ti, the discoverer, from the country as a dangerous man. Sure enough one of his successors went to the bad by giving way to drink.

It is said that silver was minted and used in this reign, barter having been previously employed.

One of the interesting subjects that chance to come under the purview of the man who studies Chinese matters and makes them a speciality may be here noted. At first sight the ordinary man would scarcely think that the researches of Sven Heden, the celebrated traveller in Central Asia, would have much to do with things Chinese; but one of the main objects which Dr. Heden had in view 'was to solve the important question of the drainage of Eastern Turkestan and throw light on the baffling problem of Lake Lop—a question which for twenty centuries has sought a satisfactory solution.' Now it is interesting to note that the first mention historically of this lake is in the ancient Chinese Classic, the 'Shi King,' 'where the traveller Chang-kien describes it under the simple name of the "Salt March." This was in the 2nd century B.C. Its traditional history goes back many centuries further, prior indeed to the establishment of the Chinese State.' Again this Lake Lop is mentioned in the 'Lesser Han Shü' 'under the name of the Pok-chang, apparently for Bogshahr' and it was then larger than in modern times. It was still larger when spoken of in the ancient Chinese Classic. In that book it is referred to in the tribute of Yü and was then known as the Yok-shui which the Chinese have translated as the 'weak water' and it was described as being so weak that the water could not support a feather's weight even. It has been suggested that it should be rendered not as weak water, but as 'dead', or 'dying'; and so its gradual absorption was even then going on thousands of years ago. In fact at 'a still earlier date geology teaches us the lake was a vast inland sea, the last remains of a former Asiatic Mediterranean' and as the learned sinologue who has called attention lately to the subject says 'the survival of these ancient legends seems to testify to the contemporaneity of the last stage with the human occupation of Central Asia.'

The whole population of China was only between one and two millions at this time. In fact the Chinese people did not at any time number more than 60,000,000 till the end of the seventeenth century. We must not suppose that the whole of what we know as modern China was ancient China.

The ancient Chinese had then come from the province of Shan-si and the Yellow River eastwards to Shan-tung, westwards to Sz-chuen, and southwards to the Yang-tsz. The country was divided into nine provinces, while the Chinese were like colonists scattered amongst the aborigines. The land along the Yellow River and the province of Honan was fairly brought under the cultivation of civilised man; but other parts were overrun with luxuriant vegetation—overgrown with jungle—thick jungle, the lair of wild beasts; for birds and beasts swarmed, as they always will in a tropical land if man does not deprive them of all their shelter Those of us who have lived long at the Peak here in Hong Kong have noticed that with the growth of the trees in the valleys, stretching from the heights to the lower levels, that the number of our songsters have increased appreciably.

Roads there were none; there were the tracks of the wild beasts through forest and wood, through the long grass and undergrowth of brushwood. These tracks when convenient formed the paths by which the first Chinaman would find his way to the brooklet, or stream, or his wife would follow them up the mountain-side, perhaps grass-cutting to feed the kitchen-fire if with the plentiful trees they did not use wood in those days. One is inclined to wonder whether the narrowness of those primitive ways led the Chinese to that curious habit they have of walking in Indian file, no matter how wide the road may be, or whether it was economy of space in the rice-field and the narrow ledge of dried mud was all that could be spared, or again whether the lanes, which take the place of streets in the South, at all events, are responsible for the habit. Be that as it may, one cannot help thinking that the primitive Chinaman just copied the elephant, rhinoceros, the tiger, lion, and tapir's tracks, and where they were not distinct enough, or where there were none, it was easy enough for him to make a road—for roads are easily made in China. Euclid's definition of a line—length without breadth—would apply pretty well to a Chinese path. Roads are indeed easily made in this land, which one is almost inclined to call a land of no roads—all that is necessary is for a sod to be cut out, then another next it and so on in a line, not always straight by any means; for the path seems most perversely to take full advantage of every twist and turn possible, and then heigh-presto, there is your ready-made road. A lady said to me the other day that Hong Kong was so curly. I don't know about that; but those of you who know what Chinese roads are will agree that they are curly enough. The description applied to a certain school of art would fit them well, viz.,—'the concentrated essence of a wriggle.' Thus then you have your road, good enough for a sparsely inhabited country district, whilst instead of a roller, scores or hundreds of naked feet, with their constant tread, soon reduce it to more or less of smoothness, treading it down with their soft patter as they go to or from their daily toil. The road is widened as necessity arises, and, if a main artery through the country, even paved with slabs of granite, or blocks of concrete. This in the South; in the North the exigencies of vehicular traffic demand a somewhat different style.

The early Chinese, what with the aborigines and what with the wild beasts, had their energies taxed to the full; and their patient labour and persistent efforts, their untiring toil were, if not called out by their environment, materially developed by it. The aborigines were gradually ousted from the portions desired by John Chinaman's ancestors: and though they did not completely drive them out of the land—for they remain to this day somewhat of a thorn in their sides—they were often relegated to mountain districts from which rocky fastnesses they defied the conquering race. These primitive races are worthy of more study than they have received in the past. They are more of Nature's children than the Chinese are.

A lot of legendary tales are crystallised round the ancient worthies. Take the time of Yau and Shun for example. In those good times (How the Chinese have deteriorated, according to their own standard!!!) everyone was so honest that doors and windows were not closed at night, and anything dropped on the road was left till the owner returned for it. Then the emperor Shun was such a filial son that the wild beasts in recognition of it, came voluntarily and drew his plough for him and the birds of the air kept watch over his grain to keep the insects from stealing it. One wonders whether, when the birds were tired, the insects watched the birds to keep them from taking it or why the birds were so honest and good to him, and the only answer we get is that his virtue was so great that it even moved the animal creation to admiration. But why in that case were the insects also not affected by it? In those Golden Ages it was sufficient to draw a circle round your prisoner and there he was. He was so good, he never thought of crossing the line; it was to him as prison walls and iron bars. The poet was right enough when he said:—

> 'Stone walls do not a prison make,
>
> Or iron bars a cage.'

But why when everyone was so good they ever needed to make a man a prisoner is one of those mysteries one would like to have explained; but it does not do to ask too many questions about those far-off times whether in the East or in the West.

I do not know whether a modern application of this same plan in Europe itself will enable us to better understand this primitive prison-plan in far Cathay. It is as follows:—The principal public square of Cettinje, the capital of Montenegro is the gaol. Here the prisoners confined for minor offences 'are allowed to roam about the square at will, the mere fact that they have been deprived of their weapons being considered appropriate punishment. At night the prisoners are removed to a room in the town hall, where they have far more comfortable quarters than they would have at home. The thought of escaping seldom occurs to them, and, even if they did, there is no place where they could find refuge. The Montenegrans are, above all, men of honour, and were a prisoner to escape, the population of Cettinje would soon be at the heels of the fugitive guilty of having broken his promise not to attempt to escape.'

China has had its bad rulers as well as its good ones: its sinners as well as its saints. In B.C. 1818 Chieh-kwei and his consort spent all they extorted in unbridled volup-tuousness. A pond was made and filled with wine on which a boat could float. It was so large that 3,000 men could drink from it at once. Pyramids of delicate viands of the finest kinds surrounded this lake, and, after drinking, those who had drunk were allowed to attack them. To cap all this extravagance and gluttony the wildest orgies were held in the Palace. It would be hard to beat the following for wanton cruelty:—It is recorded of the last of the Shang dynasty that he and his Empress noticed several women gathering shellfish bare-legged, on a river's bank one winter's morn-ing, and, like some of us, they wondered how they could stand the cold when others shivered, even in the warmest clothing. But, not content with wondering, they had their legs cut off to see the marrow of those who were so insusceptible to cold. This same Emperor had the heart of a bold official brought to him that he might see the difference between the heart of one who dared to reprove him and that of a cowardly minister. Even in an Eastern country like China, with the long forbearance of the populace, such things would not be endured by the people.

Yet in those early days there was an advanced state of civilisation. 'There was a reasonable security of life and property. The people lived in well-built houses; they dressed in silk or homespun; they wore shoes of leather; they carried unbrellas; they sat on chairs and used tables; they rode in carts and chariots; they travelled by boat; and they ate their food off plates and dishes of pottery, coarse perhaps, yet still superior to the wooden trencher, common not so very long ago in Europe. They measured time by the sundial.'

The Chinese are not content with a genuine and wonderful antiquity for many of their inventions and dis-coveries; but they push them back to a prehistoric period where we are unable to follow them. China's Cadmus is a person called Ts'ang Chieh who took the idea of a written language from the imprint of birds' claws on the sand. No wonder that with such a wonderful discovery the heavens rained grain and the evil spirits mourned by night. Nor is it very surprising to find this man blessed with four eyes. Nowadays a four-eyed man means a man who wears glasses; but the chronicles of that time are too sober for us to put that construction on the phrase; and in fact spectacles are said to be quite a modern convenience copied from the foreigner. Some of the Chinese gods are blessed with three eyes. Our scientists say that ages ago, countless ages ago, our progenitors in the scale of existence had an eye in the forehead where the third eye of the Chinese god appears. One wonders whether the two have any connection.

Before this invention of the four-eyed man, knotted cords were the means of recording events, as in modern times in ancient Mexico and by their quippu with the native Peruvians. It is said that the Chinese used little cords with sliding knots in transacting business, and yet we do not read of business getting into a tangled mess. One is inclined to suppose that these cords and knots must be the origin of the abacus in such common use by the Chinese and also employed in our western lands to teach our youngsters their arithmetic. After the knotted cords the Chinese advanced, like some other races, to the notched-stick state to convey their ideas. And then we come to rude outlines of natural objects. With the savage nations of the west—our forefathers—the picture writing developed from the first attempts at art by prehistoric man in the stone age into an alphabet. Sir John Lubbock (Lord Avebury) says the method probably would be that the drawings would come to represent first a word and then a sound, being at the same time simplified and conventionalised. The Chinese, however, developed in another direction—they did not go on to the alphabetical stage, but were content first with the pictorial state. In course of time they found this was not sufficient and it was developed along certain lines, somewhat changing its hieroglyphic form. The study of hieroglyphics is, of course, very fascinating and there is enough of the picture writing left in the Chinese language to repay one for the trouble taken over it. I do not know whether you have read, those of you who have children, Rudyard Kipling's 'Just So Stories.' It is a clever book and one of the best chapters in it is that entitled 'The First Letter.' In it a bright, little, prehistoric, neolithic maiden, a companion to her father while he is spearing fish, has her inventive faculties awakened by her father's spear breaking, and a stranger savage opportunely turning up, she employs

him as a messenger to take a bark letter, the first letter
ever written in the world, to her mother for her to send
another spear to her father. She draws her father with
the broken spear and the spare spear wanted. She draws
this last spear several times over, as it is so important you
see. One time unfortunately she makes it almost sticking
in her father's back. A line winds round one side of the
sketch to show her messenger the path he is to take, and as
it passes a swamp with a lot of beavers, she drags these
animals into the sketch as well, with their heads peeping
out of the water; but unfortunately they look more like
savages than beavers; and herself, owing to her lack of
skill as a draughtswoman, she puts in just behind her father,
with her hair all standing on end, as if galvanised with an
electric shock. As you may now well imagine instead of
the simple request for a spear being understood by her
mother, the whole tribe are aroused by this fearsome epistle
and think her father is being set upon by another tribe
and murdered: so his own tribe come in full strength to
his rescue. Whether the originators of Chinese hieroglyphics made such blunders or not one cannot say; but
this fertile production of Kipling's brain shows to us the
unfortunate limitations of picture-writing. Whether
from this or other causes the Chinese pressed on to a more
advanced stage and a more complex system. It is still
possible to study the modifications, or at least some of
those that the Chinese introduced and some of the different
combinations that they adopted, as they developed their
written language. Some of these picture-words when
explained to one seem plain and clear enough; but it is
questionable if when they first came into use they were as
readable as some people try to make out. Now we have no
specimens of such very primitive writing as that of the
prehistoric, neolithic Indian maiden's; for the samples
that the Chinese have preserved in their books show a
much more advanced stage when the hieroglyphics are
written, not as pictures, but in lines as writing, and a
conventionalised uniformity has been adopted for each word.

It has been said of Chinese that there is no doubt
that it is the most ancient language now spoken, and along
with the Egyptian and cuneiform amongst the oldest of
written languages, used by man. The Ethioptie and
Coptic, the Sanscrit, the Syriac, Aramaic, and Pehlevic have

all become dead languages; and the Greek, Latin, and Persian now spoken differ so much from the ancient style as to require special study to understand the books written in them; while during successive eras the written and spoken languages of the Chinese have undergone comparitively few alterations, and done much to deepen the broad line of demarcation between them and other branches of the human race.

The pictorial character of a part of the language is somewhat obscured by the change that took place in the writing materials. At first paper had not been discovered and our early Chinaman used bamboo tablets and a sharp stylus to scratch his words on the hard bamboo. What wonder then that when he invented paper he took the ubiquitous bamboo and used it to manufacture it with. Now as to 'the invention of paper we have just recently had a most interesting confirmation of its ancient discovery. The Chinese invention of paper has received additional confirmation from Sven Heden, who, on his recent journeys found Chinese paper that dates back to the second half of the third century after Christ. This lay buried in the sand of the Gobi Desert, near the former shore of the Lop Nor Sea, where, in the ruins of a city, and in the remnants of one of the oldest houses, he discovered a number of manuscripts, many of paper covered with Chinese script for some 1,650 years. According to Chinese sources paper was manufactured as early as the second millennium before the Christian era. The character of the newly found manuscript, makes it probable that paper making from vegetable fibres was already an old art in the third century A.D.'

But before his paper was invented John Chinaman wrote on silk, as he does to this day when he wants to specially honour anyone with a gift of his scrolls. It was a long time after the invention of paper that he discovered how to make his cakes of ink, which our fellow-countrymen will persist in calling Indian ink.

The most of the Chinese dynasties begin with splendid specimens of what a ruler ought to be, then they tail down into weaklings or cruel brutes. In the East we get a counterpart of the West; in the West we have a replica of the East. As one writer has well said:—'How few great fathers have had great sons! How often, on the contrary, is the son

:a mockery of the father's character! Marcus Aurelius is succeeded by a Commodus; at the dawn of the Middle Ages Clovis in the West and Heraclius in the East, doughty warriors themselves, are each followed by a long line of incompetents; Cromwell is succeded by the weakling Richard.'

A sovereign, who reigned from 1,198 to 1,194 B.C, is credited with having first invented idols. He did this to show his utter disbelief in any religion. He looked upon Heaven and the spirits of the mountains and streams, reverenced by the people, as mythical, and, to show contempt for such divinities, he had figures made in wood and clay to represent them. He then made some of the people fight with them; the people of course, came off victorious, when Wu-yih the Emperor, told them that this was proof that they were stronger than the gods they worshipped, so it would be folly for them to trust in them any more.

One of the most interesting things to notice about this time is the compass—the mariner's compass. With the Chinese it points to the south instead of to the north as with us. At first they did not think of applying it to navigation. One writer says:—'As to one thing there can be no doubt; the Chinese did not learn the properties of a magnetised needle from any other country. They found it for themselves, though it is impossible to point to the man by name who first observed that a magnetised needle points north and south.' The first mention of the south-pointing needle is by a Chinese author, who lived in the fourth century B.C. Another writer says of the compass:—'China's claim to the discovery of the mariners' compass is uncontested. The magnet was known at an early epoch to both Greeks and Egyptians; the former gave it its name, and the latter according to Plutarch, employed it as a symbol for a good man, who not only attracts others but possesses the power of imparting his virtue. Yet the first to observe its directive properties were the Chinese. By them the polarity of the needle was utilised long before the Christian era. Some of their books assert that it was used to guide war-chariots across a desert as early as 2,600 B.C., but the war is legendary and the assertion groundless. More within range is their unvarying statement, that magnetised needles were given to ambassadors from a southern country to enable them to find their way home, 1,100 B.C. These ambassadors came by land, and from its use in their vehicles the compass came to be described as *chih-nan-ch'e*, a south-pointing-chariot. A curious illustration of that primitive application of the needle may be seen any day, in a small compass suspended in the sedan or cart of a mandarin. The use of the needle at sea follows as a matter of course. The Chinese employed it in coasting voyages as early as the fifth century A.D. and it is probable that their junks as well as their land carriages were provided with it long before that date. Its use was known in Europe as early as the twelfth century, and possibly much earlier, the crusades, which mingled all nations, having served to propagate the arts of the East—but it was slow in coming into vogue. In the bold hands of Columbus, three centuries later, it pointed the way to a new world. Yet Vasco da Gama seems to have made little or no use of it in his voyage to India in 1,497, which was in fact a coasting voyage all the way. Camoëns, in his poetical narrative, "Os Lusiades," though he praises the astrolabe and is ever on the alert for things marvellous and strange, makes no allusion to the needle.' The intense interest of such a subject to us, a maritime nation, must be my excuse for such a long quotation. The compass first used by the Chinese had a floating needle.

Though the founders of the Chaú dynasty, Man Wong, Mò Wong, and Chaú Kung, were among the most distinguished men of antiquity for erudition, integrity, patriotism, and inventions, a grave political mistake was made by Mò Wong in dividing the empire up into petty states. The central authority was weakened by this, as well as by another cause, and a multiplicity of feudal states grew up, as many as 125 at one time, little kingdoms themselves, the weaker succumbing to the stronger and all belittling the authority of the ruling sovereign. It was during the time of these feudal states and amidst all this confusion and strife that two of the most remarkable men that China has ever produced came into the world—Lao-tsz and Confucius— nor must one forget the other great sage of that age, Mencius. It is impossible in the short space of an hour's lecture to present a true picture of Confucius and the system which has grown up round his instructions as a nucleus. Confucianism is so blended with nearly all that concerns China that one scarcely knowns where to begin or where to leave off in an attempt at a description which almost baffles description in an intelligible manner to Western ears and comprehension. To try and condense Confucianism into one single sentence, one may say that it is a system of philosophy, or ethics, and ceremonial observances to which its founder and followers ascribed the highest possibilities if carried out rigidily and faithfully to every minute jot and tittle. This belief is beginning to be shaken with the new era on which China is entering. Now Confucianism is scarcely a religion. 'It is a system of social and political morality,' while 'Taoism embraces the primitive religion of China,' a multitude of superstitions, 'and all the intellectual tendencies which did not find satisfaction in Confucianism.'

It is in only comparatively recent times amongst us in the West that folk-lore, especially the gathering together of folk-songs has taken place. Now Confucius made a collection of ancient folk-songs of China several centuries before the Christian era, and they form one of the Classical works of the Chinese.

Lao-tsz, the founder of Taoism, left nothing behind him but a small book of five thousand words. To the Western reader the book is one of the most delightful of Chinese books of that class. It seems to approach nearer to the grand truths so magnificently expressed in parts of our own incomparable Bible. Its diction is simple; its sentences terse; its style enigmatic. On such a slender base as this has been erected a superstructure, which on account of its disproportionate foundation has been compared to an inverted pyramid; but this afterday development of Taoism is a mass of the grossest superstition. Were we to follow Taoism down the centuries of Chinese history, we should find that the alchemy of the middle ages of Europe was to a great extent but a replica of the doings of the Chinese. In Europe alchemy developed into chemistry; in China it did not arrive at that stage; but before we deride the Chinese for their want of enterprise in this direction, let us not forget that there is a suspicion that the alchemy of the West was derived from the Chinese. The elixir of immortality, and the philosopher's stone, to say the least of it, are common both to the East and the West. And here let me remark that it is curious how we are prone to pick out the differences between our neighbours and ourselves instead of the points of resemblance. Especially is this the case with our view of things Chinese. And it is generally the comical side which we select to look at; the Chinese also see what seems to them our grotesque ways. It perhaps might not be amiss if we both studied each other, more often than we do, from the points of resemblance, and the more one knows of the Chinese do these similarities between our two civilisations, manners and customs, and modes of thought come into prominence and notice; so that one sees how much the Chinese are like ourselves in many things, though at first they appear to be so entirely different from us.

Millions were slain during the constant wars which lasted during the whole of the Chaú dynasty; but out of all this continued strife between the feudal princes themselves and between them and their own subjects grew the material out of which a greater China was to be established, for before the Chaú, China was without doubt but of limited extent. The end of that dynasty saw the southern border-line of the Chinese empire extended to the south of the Yang-tsz.

Let me pause here to point out an important invention. Twenty-one centuries ago the iron needle was first used. Before that, as far as needles were concerned, China was in a neolithic age. Every woman needs a needle and stone needles supplied the wants of the Chinese women. This invention must have prepared the way eventually for the beautiful embroidery the Chinese are so skilful at making.

From 220 to 204 B.C. we have Ts'in-shih Huang-ti who consolidated the empire and divided it into thirty-six provinces. He has been called the Napoleon of China, and was the builder of the Great Wall, the constructor of palaces, public edifices, canals, and roads. The latter, like the old Roman roads in England, remain to this day. Though a man of consummate skill and ability, the Chinese have nothing but ill to say of him; for one act of his has blasted him to all eternity in their eyes; and this was the destruction of all the classical works and the slaughter of five hundred scholars. He wished to blot out, for one thing, all records of a former China and start afresh with himself as the first emperor, as well as to keep the conceited Chinese scholars in check. Now here comes the wonderful part of the thing, and that is that though the books were burned, or rather their contents, they were not destroyed; for it was impossible for this despot to make a clean slate of the memories of the scholars of China. Centuries of memorising and conceutration of study had so developed the faculty of retaining and reproducing what had been so well learned that the minds of these Chinese scholars, and of the whole race evidently as well, had become, and the Chinese mind is still, a retentive vehicle of transmission. The grand old Chinese Classics were recovered in their entirety. A few copies were also found hidden in walls of houses.

This monarch's son reigned but seven years and the short-lived dynasty came to an end as well as the ancient history of China.

We now come to the glorious Hán dynasty. The Napoleon of China had established centralised power, and started a line of autocratic sovereigns, which, notwithstanding numerous revolutions, is to this day the bond of the empire.

The Hán dynasty is glorious from a literary, historical, military, commercial, and artistic point of view. Competitive examinations were first started and have lasted to the present time. It has even been said by some that the system of competitive examinations now in vogue amongst us was copied in principle from that of the Chinese.

A penal code was drawn up which has formed the model for all subsequent ones, for with each change of dynasty a new code is prepared, and now as a sign of further progress there is to be a still newer one, founded on that of Japan, or built up on the substratum of English law.

The provinces of Fokien, Yunnan, and Canton were added to the empire, as well as the greater part of the province of Szchuen.

Chinese armies marched across Asia.

Even in the Hán dynasty some idea of the earth moving and not being a stationary object, had apparently penetrated to this empire, so remote from the rest of the stirring world. Probably this knowledge came from the West to China and we have a word meaning a chariot applied to the revolving earth.

Amongst the most noteworthy events of this period, however, was the introduction of Buddhism, frought with both good and evil to this mighty empire. A. D. 61 is the date of its introduction. The emperor dreamed that he saw a gigantic image of gold and sent to India to enquire into the character of this religion, and to obtain books and teachers of it. Buddhism came as a complement to Confucianism and Taoism. Its success was remarkable. Confucianism appeals to morality and conduct; Taoism was materialistic; and Buddhism was orginally metaphysical. At the same time, though antagonistic in many respects, and though persecution has raged against Buddhism, it is curious to notice how there is at all events, an outward pax at the present time.

Very ridiculous are the accounts given in papers and in some books of the number of Buddhists in the world. They are utterly unreliable, for to begin with, no one can tell the number of Buddhists in China. It is impossible to find out; for the eclectic nature of the Chinese, with regard to religion, precludes the possibility of forming any trustworthy estimate. In England we can arrive at some idea, though perhaps not strictly accurate, as to the religious persuasions of our people, but the difficulty would be considerably increased, if it were not an insuperable one, if the English were agnostics and at the same time Episcopalians, and also at the same time Nonconformists. You say the thing would be impossible, and yet nearly as absurd a condition of things prevails in China. For every Chinaman, who is not a Mahommedan, or Christian, is a Confucianist and at the same time very likely a Buddhist and a Taoist. There has been a mechanical combination of the three, not a chemical union where they unite as it were, to form a new religion. But it must be remembered that underlying all this there is what may be compared to the bed-rock of Chinese beliefs, and that is ancestor worship. This is very interesting to the antiquary, for ancestor worship is a widely distributed form of religion. It is a persistent survival of an old world belief, and we have in China the opportunity of studying this curious form of worship at first hand.

Sir John Lubbock (Lord Avebury) has a few interesting remarks on ancestor worship, which, owing to many persons trying to make out that this form of adoration is not worship, are worth quoting:—He says:—'The idol usually assumes the human form, and idolatry is closely connected with the form of religion which consists in the worship of ancestors;' and he goes on to say, 'We have already seen how imperfectly man realises the conception of death; and we cannot wonder that death and sleep should long have been intimately connected together in the human mind. The savage, however, knows well that in sleep the spirit lives, even though the body appears to be dead. Morning after morning he wakes himself, and sees others rise from sleep. Naturally therefore he endeavours to rouse the dead. Nor can we wonder at the very general custom of providing food and other necessaries for the use of the dead. Among races leading a settled and quiet life this habit would tend to continue longer and longer. [We thus see a reason why it has lasted so long amongst the Chinese.] Prayers to the dead would reasonably follow from such customs, for even without attributing a greater power to the dead than to the living, they might yet, from their different sphere and nature, exercise a considerable power, whether good or evil.' [And now I wish to call your particular attention to this last sentence that I shall read]:—'But it is impossible to distinguish a request to an invisible being from prayer; or a powerful spirit from a demi-god.' There is no doubt that at first sight there is a little apparent difficulty to those who may turn their attention to this curious survival of the customs of savage man. For one thing the same word is used for 'reverence' and 'worship' amongst the Chinese, and the two run by such almost imperceptible gradations from one to the other that it is difficult to pronounce off hand at times an opinion on certain acts; but I think nearly all who have gone carefully into the subject will quite agree with the opinion of Lord Avebury as to its being worship. I do not think there need be the slightest doubt on the subject. If the ancestor-worship of the Chinese is not worship, then the Chinese do not worship at all. The prayers are of the same nature and kind as those offered to the idols and so are the offerings themselves. I may just finish what I have to say on this subject by noting that Professor Giles of Cambridge, whom possibly some of us knew when he was a consul, or consul-general, in China, says in one of his latest books, after quietly and calmly putting the question before his readers:—'But I feel bound to say that in my opinion these ancestral observances can only be regarded, strictly speaking, as worship and as nothing else.'

While on the subject of religion one may just say that amongst this ancient nation are to be still found many persistent survivals of other old world religions and myths handed down from generation to generation through the long ages past. The worship of Heaven and Earth, of mountains and rivers, is still in existence, and traces of Sabianism are to be found; the adoration of trees and the planting of them near temples can be seen to this day; and a most common worship is that of stones, besides an ever present and most profound belief in evil spirits which cause disease.

One of the most interesting periods of Chinese history is that of the Three States (A.D. 220-277). It has been immortalised and a halo of romance thrown over it by one of the most famous of Chinese novels—a historical narrative called 'The History of the Three States.' Now the subject of Chinese novels is a very interesting one, albeit the novelist amongst the Chinese is ranked as a mere parasite of literature 'and as a consequence, authors have no desire to attach their names to such works.' 'Novel as the name of a thing came to us,' in the West, 'with the thing itself from Italy in the reign of Queen Elizabeth.' The 'thing' itself, as one writer thus calls the novel, was known in China long before the time of our good Queen Bess. 'Tell me a story is among the earliest expressions of our wants in life,' and amongst John Chinaman's numerous children this want was early expressed. 'Stories told for their own sake,' and stories furnished with morals, all doubtless held their sway over the progenitors of the seemingly phlegmatical Chinese, who will listen spell-bound to the story-tellers in the public squares and streets. The minute microscopic analysis of character, the problem, the psychological portraiture of every passing phase of emotion are, fortunately for the Chinese readers, unknown; so is the modern realistic novel of the Zola type, though some stories would be better with the deletion of a few passages. The historic novel is much prized. To the East is ascribed the first taste for the romance. A Chinese novel is generally a finished sketch in black and white—very black and very white, no softening down nor shading; the characters stand out in bold relief. The villains are as black as black can be and form the deepest background to throw into relief the virtuous hero and heroine and their friends, helpers and well-wishers. The hero is a paragon of excellence, physically, mentally, and morally. He often possess the prowess of a warrior, the intellect of a senior wrangler, while as regards the virtues, he stands at highwater mark. The heroine—but what need to describe her—it is needless to say she is charming, as seen through Chinese spectacles; her lover will generally find her—in this respect so different from the real Chinese women—so well acquainted with letters as to lift her from the position of a mere doll to that of a sensible and well-educated companion. Apparently insuperable difficulties, mysteries, wonders, and magic are not unknown, and are, of course, piled up by the novelist for him to clear away by his consummate skill in the unravelling of the plots and intrigues against hero and heroine, and again, of course, all comes well in the end.

As to Chinese literature generally:—it is impossible to touch upon it, except just to notice that there is such a thing as a vast literature. One feels inclined to say that the Chinese are nothing if they are not literary, and yet there is an immense amount of illiteracy in China as well. But there is a vast world of Chinese sages, classical authors, historians, miscellaneous writers, religious enthusiasts, lexicographists, encyclopædists, medical experts, dramatists, novelists, journalists, wits and humourists. From the feudal times to the present—from 600 B. C. till now—2,500 years, for all this long period books have poured forth from the press in this ancient Empire of Books and Literature— poured from the press, ever since there was a printing press to multiply them (A.D. 940); and, before that, laboriously copied by loving hands, albeit they were those of the 'yellow man,' just as in the early days of literary efforts in our Western Worlds of Letters the modern press and publishers had their prototypes in scribes, monks, and copyists.

So celebrated is the Hán Dynasty in the annals of Chinese history that one of the most common names for a Chinese among themselves in the North of China is a Hán man.

We come in the T'ong Dynasty (A.D. 618-907) to another of those most illustrious periods in Chinese history which lasted for nearly 300 years, and the Chinese in the South are known as men of T'ong. Of that time it has been said that China was probably the most civilised country on the earth; the darkest days of the West, when Europe was wrapped in the ignorance and degradation of the Middle Ages, formed the brightest era of the East.

Glass has been in use in China since the time of the T‘ong Dynasty, and paper money was first used in this period.

The second emperor of this dynasty may be regarded as the most accomplished in the Chinese annals. 'His broad dominions extended to the borders of Persia and the Caspian Sea, embracing large parts of Central Asia.'

Mahommedanism was introduced into China six years after the hegira of the Prophet. There are supposed to be from 20,000,000 to 25,000,000 Moslems in China at the present time.

'The balance as to priority (in the discovery of gunpower) appears to be in favour of China, and cannon were used in the siege of T‘ai Yuan in A.D. 767. The first incontestable use of cannon in Europe was in A.D. 1338.'

This was a great period for Chinese poets, 'and a complete collection of the works of the epoch are arranged in 48,900 pieces in 900 books.' It would take a life-time to read them. The best translator of Chinese poetry thus writes about it:—'A long poem does not appeal to the Chinese mind. There is no such thing as an epic in the language, though, of course, there are many pieces extending to several hundred lines. Brevity is indeed the soul of a Chinese poem, which is valued not so much for what it says as' for what it does not say, or rather it is valued not so much for what it says as 'for what it suggests. As in painting, so in poetry suggestion is the end and aim of the artist, who in each case may be styled an impressionist. The ideal length is twelve lines, and this is the limit set to candidates at the great public examinations at the present day, the Chinese holding that if a poet cannot say within such compass what he has to say it may very well be left unsaid. The eight-line poem is also a favourite, and so, but for its extreme difficulty, is the four line epigram, or stopshort;' so called, as the critics explain, because 'it is only the words which stop, the sense goes on, some train of thought having been suggested to the reader. The latter form of verse was in use as far back as the Hán dynasty, but only reached perfection under the T‘ongs.'

It is in the T'ong dynasty that the invention of print-ing took place; it was suggested by rubbings being taken of the Classics cut in stone.

The Sung (A.D. 960-1126) is another of the great dynasties of Chinese history. There was a greater con-centration of power in the Supreme Government, the almost autocratic authority of the Governors of the pro-vinces being curtailed. 'The period is noted for its literary men, especially for Chü-hei, the great commentator on the Chinese Classics, whose interpretations have totally obli-terated those of the scholars of the Hán, and have been the sole and only Confucian orthodoxy ever since, a literary triumph which for thoroughness and permanence has few parallels in history,' so writes one author.

It seems strange to find Socialism tried in China; but a statesman made the attempt to find it not succeed.

The 'Three Character Classic,' read as his first lesson book by nearly every Chinese boy when he first goes to school, was written during the Sung dynasty, 800 years ago.

The last prince of the Sungs encamped in the New Territory of Hongkong, and the memory of this event is recorded on a large boulder, this side of Kaú Lung City and on the opposite side of the road, to the Church Mission Chapel, lately built.

For centuries the Chinese had almost constant con-flicts with the Tartar tribes, who, under one name or another, ravaged their borders and harassed them almost beyond endurance, taking at times part of the empire to them-selves. Eventually two of these nomadic tribes obtained rule over China. The Mongols, one of them, (A.D. 1260-1341) was the first. Of course, the Mongol sway was a foreign one to the Chinese. This period is interesting to us, as being that when the great mediæval traveller, Marco Polo, visited far off Cathay, and described in his gossipy, but wonderfully truthful pages, the vast domains and the splendour of the Court of the Khan at Peking, which was made the capital for the first time. Ghengis Khan and Kublai Khan are names connected with this epoch of Chinese history. It is interesting at the present moment to note that Kublai Khan made two invasions of Japan, but both times without success; for, as in the case of the in-vasion of our own coasts by the great Spanish Armada, the elements seemed to be allies with the invaded nation against the invaders. 13,000 men are said to have perished on the side of the Mongols in the first attempt, and 100,000 Mongols and 7,000 Coreans on the second occasion. After 89 years of the Mongol rule we get a native dynasty again under the Mings (A.D. 1368-1628).

At the command of Yung-lo, one of the Ming emperors, a gigantic encyclopædia was prepared, putting quite into shade, as far as regards size, the 'Times' latest production in that direction. Over two thousand scholars were engaged in the task. It was contained in 22,877 volumes, the table of contents occupying 60 books. Of this enormous book only two copies were ever made. The one was destroyed in a fire in Nanking, and the other, as doubtless you know, at the siege of the legations in Peking. Of this last copy, several hundred volumes were rescued, it is said, and are now scattered over the broad world in the possession of the curious.

It was during the time of the Mings that the neighbouring colony of Macao came into the hands of the Portuguese; and it was also during the same dynasty that the first Jesuit missionaries came to China.

And now at last we come to the foreign rulers of present China. In the case of the Chinese and the Manchus, history repeated itself; for it was not the most warlike race that really triumphed in the long run. Someone has said— in fact one of our warlike Japanese, (Kanzo Uchimura by name):—'No nation has ever prospered by war alone. The ancient Sythians were simply warlike people, terrible in war, but in nothing else. They came as a storm, and as they swept over Western Asia, Assyria itself was not able to withstand their fearful onslaught. But as a storm they spent themselves in devastation. They conquered only to die. Warlike Assyrians were never such permanent conquerors as comparatively peace-loving Babylonians. Athens was no equal of Sparta on the field of battle, but it was after all, the former that conquered the world. The valour of Attila and Genseric vanished like a mirage, because they knew not how to till and build. The Dutch were greater in fighting with the North Sea than with Spaniards; and so they overcame and still survive. And the greatness of the Anglo-Saxons, with all their hypocrisies and latent paganisms, lies in their ability to handle the axe and plough. The Anglo-Saxons farmers are the mightiest conquerors on the face of the globe. French and Germans can beat them on the battlefield, but not in African jungles and American prairies. Englishmen are possessing the earth more by the might of their axes and ploughs than by that of cruisers and battleships.' But our Japanese author has overlooked one significant fact and that is that in the Anglo-Saxon race, notwithstanding all their hypocrisies, as he calls them, in this the most enlightened and civilised branch of the human family on the face of the globe, Christianity has the fullest sway, and the most degraded nations, on the other hand, are those in which Christianity is practically unknown.

Though the Manchus were the conquerors of the Chinese, yet as has happened in other parts of the world in similar cases, the conquerors have been vanquished when it came to a question of language. The Manchus, having no literature of their own, tried their best to foster the acquisition of their own language by their own people; for that purpose they had books translated from the Chinese into Manchu; but notwithstanding all their efforts it is almost practically a dead language, as far as books are concerned. The Manchus numbered 5,000,000 in 1848. Many of them are scattered about in garrisons throughout China and having, as I have already said, no indigenous literature of their own, have turned to Chinese books for what is lacking in their own language.

The Manchu has given some words to the Chinese language. In fact strange as it may appear the Chinese is indebted to some other languages for a few of its words. The Hán, and the T'ong, and the present dynasties are three periods in China which have been marked by a great increase in China's active relations with foreigners. Terms have been adopted from India, (Buddhism is partly responsible for that,) as well as from the Spanish, French, English, Malay, Persian, Arabic, Turkish, Mongolian, and Tibetan languages, &c. The late Mr. Watters, who wrote a most interesting book on this branch of Chinese study, I find, on counting up the results of his work, has identified 282 words as being derived from foreign languages. One must not expect, of course, to find a very large number, as we do in our own European languages; but at first sight it seems surprising to find so many, as the Chinese have kept so much to themselves in the past.

An interesting subject to enlarge upon here would be foreign influence upon China; but the subject would be a vast one if gone into fully. It appears to us, living in the midst of it, to have reached its highest development at the present time. Not the least in the factors which have produced an ardent desire for Western knowledge and science is the missionary. This is not the time or place to speak of his religious work; but I can, and do, say that the most of the Western literature, and the scientific works, which have been translated in such hundreds and thousands of volumes into Chinese, are the work of the missionary, and the Chinese are largely indebted to these ardent labourers in enlightenment, for their introduction to the wider world of Western thought and knowledge, supplemented by the schools and hospitals established by the missionary societies.

Two of the sovereigns of the present dynasty call for special attention—Kang-hsi and Chien-lung. Kang-hsi, under whose rule Formosa was conquered, the war against the Eleuths was successful, and Chinese authority became paramount in Tibet, was courageous, magnanimous, and wise and reigned for sixty-one years.

Chien-lung carried on wars against the Burmese, and the Goorkhas. He reigned for sixty years. The curious part of it to us is that he might have reigned longer; but he abdicated for the very good reason in Chinese eyes that he would be wanting in filial respect if he had remained on the throne longer than his grandfather Kang-hsi.

Europeans had arrived in China in the time of the Mings and this disturbing element, looked at from a present Chinese standpoint, still increased in numbers in the present dynasty.

The great T'ái P'ing Rebellion is one of the most noteworthy events of this Great Ts'ing (or Pure) Dynasty, unless we ourselves are seeing a greater event happening before our very eyes, namely the salvation of China from utter ruin. During the time of the Mings the Chinese had worn their hair long; but with the advent of the Manchu-Tartars they were compelled to adopt the same style of dress as their conquerors. So opposed were they to this that the turbans the Amoy and Swatow men wear were said to have been adopted by them to hide the hated innovation. However, now after more than two centuries and a half the

Chinese, up to the present day, glories in his queue. Pray do not call it a pigtail. The stout horsehair bristles of our grandfathers and of our present day lawyers may be entitled to such an opprobrious epithet, but not the long, graceful, waving queues of John Chinaman, eked out with silken cords. Now it is a very natural question to ask how this curious style of dressing the hair was started. What it was that made the Tartars take to this strange head-dress. Well, the explanation seems a very remarkable one. This strange fashion is said to have arisen in this way:—'The Tartars may be said to have depended almost for their existence upon the horse; and in old pictures the Tartar is often seen curled up asleep with his horse, illustrating the mutual affection and dependence between master and beast. Out of sheer gratitude and respect for his noble ally, the man took upon himself the form of the animal, growing a queue in imitation of the horse's tail. Unsupported by any other evidence, this somewhat grotesque theory would fall to the ground. But there is other evidence of a rather striking character, which, taken in conjunction with what had been said seems to me,' says Professor Giles, 'to settle the matter. Official coats, as seen in China at the present day, are made with very peculiar sleeves, shaped like a horse's leg, and ending in what is an unmistakable hoof, completely covering the hand. These are actually known to the Chinese as "horseshoe sleeves," and encased therein, a Chinaman's arms certainly look very much like a horse's forelegs. The tail completes the picture.'

Just as one example of the numerous highly interesting problems which present themselves to us in connection with China and the different nations which have surrounded it, one may call attention to the recent discovery of the fact that as has been stated, 'a great empire' evidently 'formerly had its seat in Manchuria centuries ago. This prehistoric race had great coal-mining engineering skill.' One would like to know a little more about this and whether it was really a prehistoric race, or whether these mines were dug during the prosperous periods of Manchu history when this power enlarged its realms, swallowing up neighbouring states, until it extended between the Gulf of Liao-tung and the Amoor. It could not have been in a low state of civilisation then, as we are told that 'learning flourished and literature abounded.'

The last century has witnessed a period of decadence in China in some respects. In most of the dynasties to which long lines of sovereigns have belonged, the latter reigns have not come up to those of the founders of these dynasties and their immediate successors, as I have already pointed out. Whether this is a sign of the passing away of the Manchu Dynasty remains to be seen.

We hear a great deal now about the anti-foreign feeling in China. Let me close this too long lecture by some signs of progress in the contrary direction which have just lately came under my immediate notice :—In October, 1904, I travelled some 450 miles away from Hongkong up the West River accomplishing on the round trip between 900 and 1,000 miles, going part of the time in native steam-launches and being in Chinese cities amongst the people themselves. Everywhere I met with the utmost civility and politeness, though I visited places which a few years ago were rabidly anti-foreign. In one city where I spent two or three days, foreigners were hounded out of the place a number of years ago and their goods and effects were thrown into the river. In another city which was very anti-foreign, I made a circuit of the city walls alone, walking through the streets and passing the night surrounded by Chinese in perfect safety. Nearly all the hatred of the foreigner has died down in that part of the country, and a great factor in producing this wonderful change, I was told, was what I am sure will be gratifying to residents in this Colony; for it was largely the result of sending relief from Hongkong a few years ago when these districts of country were famine-stricken. This timely charity in a season of dire distress showed to these people more plainly than any amount of words could that the erstwhile-hated foreigner was their friend and well-wisher and was ready to do his best to save them and theirs from starvation and death. One hopes that the persistent display of kindness on our part to the Chinese will ere long break down the remaining distrust and prejudice of us in other parts of the country; and that this prejudice and ill-will gone, China, which was for many centuries the leading power in the Far East and the centre of light and civilisation to all the surrounding nations, may be even more willing to learn than she is at present, or has been in the past, from the present-day more advanced nations of the West. Is she to waken from her lethargy and take the place her history all down the long centuries entitles her to; is she again to scatter light and knowledge among her neighbours; is she to be once more the centre of the Far East; is she to live up to her great possibilities? It needs a prophet's foresight, peering through the dark unknown future, to say whether this shall be so or not.

INDEX.